1 3 5 7 9 10 8 6 4 2

Vintage
20 Vauxhall Bridge Road,
London SW1V 2SA

Vintage Classics is part of the Penguin Random House
group of companies whose addresses can be found at
global.penguinrandomhouse.com.

Penguin
Random House
UK

First published in Great Britain by The Hogarth Press in 1959
This short edition published by Vintage in 2017

penguin.co.uk/vintage

A CIP catalogue record for this book is available from the British Library

ISBN 9781784872922

Typeset in 9.5/14.5 pt FreightText Pro
by Jouve (UK), Milton Keynes
Printed and bound by Clays Ltd, St Ives plc

Penguin Random House is committed to a sustainable future for
our business, our readers and our planet. This book is made from
Forest Stewardship Council® certified paper.

MIX
Paper from
responsible sources
FSC
www.fsc.org
FSC® C018179

Summer

LAURIE LEE

VINTAGE MINIS

I WAS SET down from the carrier's cart at the age of three; and there with a sense of bewilderment and terror my life in the village began.

The June grass, amongst which I stood, was taller than I was, and I wept. I had never been so close to grass before. It towered above me and all around me, each blade tattooed with tiger-skins of sunlight. It was knife-edged, dark, and a wicked green, thick as a forest and alive with grasshoppers that chirped and chattered and leapt through the air like monkeys.

I was lost and didn't know where to move. A tropic heat oozed up from the ground, rank with sharp odours of roots and nettles. Snow-clouds of elder-blossom banked in the sky, showering upon me the fumes and flakes of their sweet and giddy suffocation. High overhead ran frenzied larks, screaming, as though the sky were tearing apart.

For the first time in my life I was out of the sight of humans. For the first time in my life I was alone in a world whose behaviour I could neither predict nor fathom: a world of birds that squealed, of plants that stank, of insects that sprang about without warning. I was lost and I did not expect to be found again. I put back my head and howled, and the sun hit me smartly on the face, like a bully.

From this daylight nightmare I was awakened, as from many another, by the appearance of my sisters. They came scrambling and calling up the steep rough bank, and parting the long grass found me. Faces of rose, familiar, living; huge shining faces hung up like shields between me and the sky; faces with grins and white teeth (some broken) to be conjured up like genii with a howl, brushing off terror with their broad scoldings and affection. They leaned over me – one, two, three – their mouths smeared with red currants and their hands dripping with juice.

'There, there, it's all right, don't you wail any more. Come down 'ome and we'll stuff you with currants.'

And Marjorie, the eldest, lifted me into her long brown hair, and ran me jogging down the path and through the steep rose-filled garden, and set me down on the cottage doorstep, which was our home, though I couldn't believe it.

That was the day we came to the village, in the summer of the last year of the First World War. To a cottage that stood in a half-acre of garden on a steep bank above a lake; a cottage with three floors and a cellar and a treasure in the walls, with a pump and apple trees, syringa and strawberries, rooks in the chimneys, frogs in the cellar, mushrooms on the ceiling, and all for three and sixpence a week.

I don't know where I lived before then. My life began on the carrier's cart which brought me up the long slow hills to the village, and dumped me in the high grass, and lost me. I had ridden wrapped up in a Union Jack to protect me from the sun, and when I rolled out of it, and stood piping loud among the buzzing jungle of that summer bank, then, I feel, was I born. And to all the rest of us, the whole family of eight, it was the beginning of a life.

But on that first day we were all lost. Chaos was come in cartloads of furniture, and I crawled the kitchen floor through forests of upturned chair-legs and crystal fields of glass. We were washed up in a new land, and began to spread out searching its springs and treasures. The sisters spent the light of that first day stripping the fruit bushes in the garden. The currants were at their prime, clusters of red, black, and yellow berries all tangled up with wild roses. Here was bounty the girls had never known before, and they darted squawking from bush to bush, clawing the fruit like sparrows.

Our Mother too was distracted from duty, seduced by the rich wilderness of the garden so long abandoned. All day she trotted to and fro, flushed and garrulous, pouring flowers into every pot and jug she could find on the kitchen floor. Flowers from the garden, daisies from the bank, cow-parsley, grasses, ferns, and leaves – they flowed in armfuls through the cottage door until its dim interior seemed entirely possessed by the world outside – a still green pool flooding with honeyed tides of summer.

I sat on the floor on a raft of muddles and gazed through

the green window which was full of the rising garden. I saw the long black stockings of the girls, gaping with white flesh, kicking among the currant bushes. Every so often one of them would dart into the kitchen, cram my great mouth with handfuls of squashed berries, and run out again. And the more I got, the more I called for more. It was like feeding a fat young cuckoo.

The long day crowed and chirped and rang. Nobody did any work, and there was nothing to eat save berries and bread. I crawled about among the ornaments on the unfamiliar floor – the glass fishes, china dogs, shepherds and shepherdesses, bronze horsemen, stopped clocks, barometers, and photographs of bearded men. I called on them each in turn, for they were the shrines and faces of a half-remembered landscape. But as I watched the sun move around the walls, drawing rainbows from the cut-glass jars in the corner, I longed for a return of order.

Then, suddenly, the day was at an end, and the house was furnished. Each stick and cup and picture was nailed immovably in place; the beds were sheeted, the windows curtained, the straw mats laid, and the house was home. I don't remember seeing it happen, but suddenly the inexorable tradition of the house, with its smell, chaos, and complete logic, occurred as though it had never been otherwise. The furnishing and founding of the house came like the nightfall of that first day. From that uneasy loneliness of objects strewn on the kitchen floor, everything flew to its place and was never again questioned.

And from that day we grew up. The domestic arrangement of the house was shaken many times, like a snow-storm toy, so that beds and chairs and ornaments swirled from room to room, pursued by the gusty energies of Mother and the girls. But always these things resettled within the pattern of the walls, nothing escaped or changed, and so it remained for twenty years.

Now I MEASURED that first growing year by the widening fields that became visible to me, the new tricks of dressing and getting about with which I became gradually endowed. I could open the kitchen door by screwing myself into a ball and leaping and banging the latch with my fist. I could climb into the high bed by using the ironwork as a ladder. I could whistle, but I couldn't lace my shoes. Life became a series of experiments which brought grief or the rewards of accomplishment: a pondering of patterns and mysteries in the house, while time hung golden and suspended, and one's body, from leaping and climbing, took on the rigid insanity of an insect, petrified as it were for hours together, breathing and watching. Watching the grains of dust fall in the sunny room, following an ant from its cradle to the grave, going over the knots in the bedroom ceiling – knots that ran like Negroes in the dusk of dawn, or moved stealthily from board to board, but which settled again in the wax light of day no more monstrous than fossils in coal.

These knots on the bedroom ceiling were the whole range of a world, and over them my eyes went endlessly voyaging in that long primeval light of waking to which a child is condemned. They were archipelagos in a sea of blood-coloured varnish, they were armies grouped and united against me, they were the alphabet of a macabre tongue, the first book I ever learned to read.

Radiating from that house, with its crumbling walls, its thumps and shadows, its fancied foxes under the floor, I moved along paths that lengthened inch by inch with my mounting strength of days. From stone to stone in the trackless yard I sent forth my acorn shell of senses, moving through unfathomable oceans like a South Sea savage island-hopping across the Pacific. Antennae of eyes and nose and grubbing fingers captured a new tuft of grass, a fern, a slug, the skull of a bird, a grotto of bright snails. Through the long summer ages of those first few days I enlarged my world and mapped it in my mind, its secure havens, its dust-deserts and puddles, its peaks of dirt and flag-flying bushes. Returning too, dry-throated, over and over again, to its several well-prodded horrors: the bird's gaping bones in its cage of old sticks; the black flies in the corner, slimy dead; dry rags of snakes; and the crowded, rotting, silent-roaring city of a cat's grub-captured carcass.

Once seen, these relics passed within the frontiers of the known lands, to be remembered with a buzzing in the ears, to be revisited when the stomach was strong. They were the first tangible victims of that destroying force whose job I knew went on both night and day, though I could never catch him at it. Nevertheless I was grateful for them. Though they haunted my eyes and stuck in my dreams, they reduced for me the first infinite possibilities of horror. They chastened the imagination with the proof of a limited frightfulness.

From the harbour mouth of the scullery door I learned the rocks and reefs and the channels where safety lay. I discovered the physical pyramid of the cottage, its stores and labyrinths, its centres of magic, and of the green, spouting island-garden upon which it stood. My Mother and sisters sailed past me like galleons in their busy dresses, and I learned the smells and sounds which followed in their wakes, the surge of breath, air of carbolic, song and grumble, and smashing of crockery.

How magnificent they appeared, full-rigged, those towering girls, with their flying hair and billowing blouses, their white-mast arms stripped for work or washing. At any moment one was boarded by them, bussed and buttoned, or swung up high like a wriggling fish to be hooked and held in their lacy linen.

The scullery was a mine of all the minerals of living. Here I discovered water – a very different element from the green crawling scum that stank in the garden tub. You could pump it in pure blue gulps out of the ground, you could swing on the pump handle and it came out sparkling like liquid sky. And it broke and ran and shone on the tiled floor, or quivered in a jug, or weighted your clothes with cold. You could drink it, draw with it, froth it with soap, swim beetles across it, or fly it in bubbles in the air. You could put your head in it, and open your eyes, and see the sides of the bucket buckle, and hear your caught breath roar, and work your mouth like a fish, and smell the lime from the ground. Substance of magic – which you could tear or wear, confine or scatter, or send down holes, but never burn or break or destroy.

The scullery was water, where the old pump stood. And it had everything else that was related to water: thick steam of Mondays edgy with starch; soapsuds boiling, bellying and popping, creaking and whispering, rainbowed with light and winking with a million windows. Bubble bubble, toil and grumble, rinsing and slapping of sheets and shirts, and panting Mother rowing her red arms like oars in the steaming waves. Then the linen came up on a stick out of the pot, like pastry, or woven suds, or sheets of moulded snow.

Here, too, was the scrubbing of floors and boots, of arms and necks, of red and white vegetables. Walk in to the morning disorder of this room and all the garden was laid out dripping on the table. Chopped carrots like copper pennies, radishes and chives, potatoes dipped and stripped clean from their coats of mud, the snapping of tight pea-pods, long shells of green pearls, and the tearing of glutinous beans from their nests of wool.

Grown stealthy, marauding among these preparations, one nibbled one's way like a rat through roots and leaves. Peas rolled under the tongue, fresh cold, like solid water; teeth chewed green peel of apples, acid sharp, and the sweet white starch of swedes. Beaten away by wet hands gloved with flour, one returned in a morose and speechless lust. Slivers of raw pastry, moulded, warm, went down in the shapes of men and women – heads and arms of unsalted flesh seasoned with nothing but a dream of cannibalism.

Large meals were prepared in this room, cauldrons of stew for the insatiate hunger of eight. Stews of all that grew on these rich banks, flavoured with sage, coloured with Oxo, and laced with a few bones of lamb. There was, it is true, little meat at those times; sometimes a pound of bare ribs for boiling, or an occasional rabbit dumped at the door by a neighbour. But there was green food of great weight in season, and lentils and bread for ballast. Eight to ten loaves came to the house every day, and they never grew dry. We tore them to pieces with their crusts still warm, and their monotony was brightened by the objects we found in them – string, nails, paper, and once a mouse; for those were days of happy-go-lucky baking. The lentils were cooked in a great pot which also heated the water for the Saturday-night baths. Our small wood-fire could heat sufficient water to fill one bath only, and this we shared in turn. Being the youngest but one, my water was always the dirtiest but one, and the implications of this privilege remain with me to this day.

WAKING ONE MORNING in the white-washed bedroom, I opened my eyes and found them blind. Though I stretched them and stared where the room should be, nothing was visible but a glare of gold, flat on my throbbing eyelids. I groped for my body and found it there. I heard the singing of birds. Yet there was nothing at all to be seen of the world save this quivering yellow light. Was I dead, I wondered? Was I in heaven? Whatever it was I hated it. I had wakened too soon from a dream of crocodiles and I was not ready for this further outrage. Then I heard the girls' steps on the stairs.

'Our Marge!' I shouted, 'I can't see nothing!' And I began to give out my howl.

A slap of bare feet slithered across the floor, and I heard sister Marjorie's giggle.

'Just look at him,' she said. 'Pop and fetch a flannel, Doth –'is eyes've got stuck down again.'

The cold edge of the flannel passed over my face showered me with water, and I was back in the world. Bed and beams, and the sun-square window, and the girls bending over me grinning.

''Oo did it?' I yelled.

'Nobody, silly. Your eyes got bunged up, that's all.'

The sweet glue of sleep; it had happened before, but somehow I always forgot. So I threatened the girls I'd bung theirs up too: I was awake, I could see, I was happy. I lay looking out of the small green window. The world outside was crimson and on fire. I had never seen it looking like that before.

'Doth?' I said, 'what's happening to them trees?'

Dorothy was dressing. She leaned out of the window,

slow and sleepy, and the light came through her nightdress like sand through a sieve.

'Nothing's happening,' she said.

'Yes it is then,' I said. 'They're falling to bits.'

Dorothy scratched her dark head, yawning wide, and white feathers floated out of her hair.

'It's only the leaves droppin'. We're in autumn now. The leaves always drop in autumn.'

Autumn? In autumn. Was that where we were? Where the leaves always dropped and there was always this smell. I imagined it continuing, with no change, for ever, these wet flames of woods burning on and on like the bush of Moses, as natural a part of this new found land as the eternal snows of the poles. Why had we come to such a place?

In the long hot summer of 1921 a serious drought hit the country. Springs dried up, the wells filled with frogs, and the usually sweet water from our scullery pump turned brown and tasted of nails. Although this drought was a relief to my family, it was a scourge to the rest of the village. For weeks the sky hung hot and blue, trees shrivelled, crops burned in the fields, and the old folk said the sun had slipped in its course and that we should all of us very soon die. There were prayers for rain; but my family didn't go, because it was rain we feared most of all.

As the drought continued, prayer was abandoned and more devilish steps adopted. Finally soldiers with rifles marched to the tops of the hills and began shooting at passing clouds. When I heard their dry volleys, breaking like sticks in the stillness, I knew our long armistice was over. And sure enough – whether from prayers or the shooting, or by a simple return of nature – the drought broke soon after and it began to rain as it had never rained before.

I remember waking in the night to the screams of our Mother, and to rousing alarms of a howling darkness and the storm-battered trees outside. Terror, the old terror, had come again, and as always in the middle of the night.

'Get up!' cried Mother. 'It's coming in! Get up or we'll all be drowned!'

I heard her banging about and beating the walls in accents of final doom. When Mother gave her alarms one didn't lie back and think, one didn't use reason at all; one just erected one's hair and leapt out of bed and scrambled downstairs with the others.

Our predicament was such that we lived at nature's mercy; for the cottage, stuck on its steep bank, stood directly in the path of the floods. All the spouts of the heavens seemed to lead to our door, and there was only one small drain to swallow them. When this drain blocked up, as it did in an instant, the floods poured into our kitchen – and as there was no back door to let them out again I felt it natural at the time we should drown.

'Hell in Heaven!' wailed Mother. 'Damn it and cuss! Jesus have mercy on us!'

We grizzled and darted about for brooms, then ran out to tackle the storm. We found the drain blocked already and the yard full of water. The noise of the rain drowned our cries and whimpers, and there was nothing to do but sweep.

What panic those middle-night rousings were, those trumpet-calls murdering sleep; with darkness, whirlwind, and invisible rain, trees roaring, clouds bursting, thunder crashing, lightning crackling, floods rising, and our Mother demented. The girls in their nightdresses held spitting candles while we boys swept away at the drain. Hot rods of rain struck straight through our shirts; we shivered with panic and cold.

'More brooms!' shouted Mother, jumping up and down. 'Run, someone, in the name of goodness! Sweep harder, boys! Sweet saints above, it's up to the doorstep already!'

The flood-water gurgled and moved thickly around us, breeding fat yellow bubbles like scum, skipping and frothing where the bullet rain hit it, and inching slowly towards the door. The drain was now hidden beneath the water and we swept at it for our lives, the wet candles hissed and went out one by one, Mother lit torches of newspapers, while we fought knee-deep in cries and thunder, splashing about, wet-through, half-weeping, overwhelmed by gigantic fears.

Sometimes, in fact, the water did get in; two or three inches of it. It slid down the steps like a thick cream custard and spread all over the floor. When that happened, Mother's lamentations reached elegiac proportions, and all the world was subpoenaed to witness. Dramatic apostrophes rang through the night; the Gods were arraigned, the Saints called to order, and the Fates severely ticked off.

There would be a horrible mess in the kitchen next morning, mud and slime all over the matting, followed by the long depressed drudgery of scraping it up and carrying it away in buckets. Mother, on her knees, would wring her hands and roll her eyes about.

'I can't *think* what I've done to be so troubled and tried. And just when I got the house straight. Neither saints nor angels would keep their patience if they had such things to put up with ... My poor, poor children, my precious darlings – you could die in this filthy hole. No one would care – not a bell-essed soul. Look out with that damn-and-cuss bucket!' . . .

Apart from the noise and the tears and the dirt, these inundations were really not much. But I can't pretend they didn't scare me stiff. The thought that the flood-waters should actually break into our house seemed to me something worse than a fire. At the mid-hour of night, when the storms really blew, I used to lie aghast in my bed, hearing the rain claw the window and the wind slap the walls, and imagining the family, the house, and all the furniture, being sucked down the eternal drain.

It was not till much later that I reasoned things out: that our position on the hillside made it unlikely we should drown, that Mother's frenzies and scares belonged to something else altogether, and that it was possible after all to sleep through rain in peace. Even so, to this day, when the skies suddenly darken, and a storm builds up in the west, and I smell rain on the wind and hear the first growl of thunder, I grow uneasy, and start looking for brooms.

WAKING UP IN the morning I saw squirrels in the yew trees nibbling at the moist red berries. Between the trees and the window hung a cloud of gold air composed of floating seeds and spiders. Farmers called to their cows on the other side of the valley and moorhens piped from the ponds. Brother Jack, as always, was the first to move, while I pulled on my boots in bed. We both stood at last on the bare-wood floor, scratching and saying our prayers. Too stiff and manly to say them out loud, we stood back to back and muttered them, and if an audible plea should slip out by chance, one just burst into song to cover it.

Singing and whistling were useful face-savers, especially when confounded by argument. We used the trick readily, one might say monotonously, and this morning it was Jack who began it.

'What's the name of the king, then?' he said, groping for his trousers.

'Albert.'

'No, it's not. It's George.'

'That's what I said you, didn't I? George.'

'No you never. You don't know. You're feeble.'

'Not so feeble as you be, any road.'

'You're balmy. You got brains of a bed-bug.'

'Da-da-di-da-da.'

'I said you're brainless. You can't even count.'

'Turrelee-turrelee . . . Didn't hear you.'

'Yes you did then, blockhead. Fat and lazy. Big faa—'

'Dum-di-dah! . . . Can't hear . . . Hey nonnie! . . .'

Well, that was all right; honours even, as usual. We broke the sleep from our eyes and dressed quickly.

Walking downstairs there was a smell of floorboards, of rags, sour lemons, old spices. The smoky kitchen was in its morning muddle, from which breakfast would presently emerge. Mother stirred the porridge in a soot-black pot. Tony was carving bread with a ruler, the girls in their mackintoshes were laying the table, and the cats were eating the butter. I cleaned some boots and pumped up some fresh water; Jack went for a jug of skimmed milk.

'I'm all behind,' Mother said to the fire. 'This wretched coal's all slack.'

She snatched up an oil-can and threw it all on the fire. A belch of flame roared up the chimney. Mother gave a loud scream, as she always did, and went on stirring the porridge.

'If I had a proper stove,' she said. 'It's a trial getting you off each day.'

I sprinkled some sugar on a slice of bread and bolted it down while I could. How different again looked the kitchen this morning, swirling with smoke and sunlight. Some cut-glass vases threw jagged rainbows across the piano's field of dust, while Father in his pince-nez up on the wall looked down like a scandalized god.

At last the porridge was dabbed on our plates from a thick and steaming spoon. I covered the smoky lumps with treacle and began to eat from the sides to the middle. The girls round the table chewed moonishly, wrapped in their morning stupor. Still sick with sleep, their mouths moved slow, hung slack while their spoon came up; then they paused for a moment, spoon to lip, collected their wits, and ate. Their vacant eyes stared straight before them, glazed at the sight of the day. Pink and glowing from their dreamy beds, from who knows what arms of heroes, they seemed like mute spirits hauled back to the earth after paradise feasts of love.

'Golly!' cried Doth. 'Have you seen the time?'

They began to jump to their feet.

'Goodness, it's late.'

'I got to be off.'

'Me too.'

'Lord, where's my things?'

'Well, ta-ta Ma; ta boys – be good.'

'Anything you want up from the Stores . . . ?'

They hitched up their stockings, patted their hats, and went running up the bank. This was the hour when walkers and bicyclists flowed down the long hills to Stroud, when the hooters called through the morning dews and factories puffed out their plumes. From each crooked corner of Stroud's five valleys girls were running to shops and looms, with sleep in their eyes, and eggy cheeks, and in their ears night voices fading. Marjorie was off to her Milliners' Store, Phyllis to her Boots-and-Shoes, Dorothy to her job as junior clerk in a decayed cloth-mill by a stream. As for Harold, he'd started work already, his day began at six, when he'd leave the house with an angry shout for the lathe-work he really loved.

But what should we boys do, now they had all gone? If it was school-time, we pushed off next. If not, we dodged up the bank to play, ran snail races along the walls, or dug in the garden and found potatoes and cooked them in tins on the rubbish heap. We were always hungry, always calling for food, always seeking it in cupboards and hedges. But holiday mornings were a time of risk, there might be housework or errands to do. Mother would be ironing, or tidying-up, or reading books on the floor. So if we hung around the yard we kept our ears cocked; if she caught us, the game was up.

'Ah, there you are, son. I'm needing some salt. Pop to Vick's for a lump, there's a dear.'

Or: 'See if Granny Trill's got a screw of tea – only ask her nicely, mind.'

Or: 'Run up to Miss Turk and try to borrow half-crown; I didn't know I'd got so low.'

'Ask our Jack, our Mother! I borrowed the bacon. It's blummin'-well his turn now.'

But Jack had slid off like an eel through the grass, making his sly get-away as usual. He was jumpy, shifty, and quick-off-the-mark, an electric flex of nerves, skinny compared with the rest of us, or what farmers might call a 'poor doer'. If they had, in fact, they would have been quite wrong, for Jack did himself very well. He had developed a mealtime strategy which ensured that he ate for two. Speed and guile were the keys to his success, and we hungry ones called him The Slider.

Jack ate against time, that was really his secret; and in our house you had to do it. Imagine us all sitting down to dinner; eight round a pot of stew. It was lentil-stew usually, a heavy brown mash made apparently of plastic studs. Though it smelt of hot stables, we were used to it, and it was filling enough – could you get it. But the size of our family out-stripped the size of the pot, so there was never quite enough to go round.

When it came to serving, Mother had no method, not even the law of chance – a dab on each plate in any old order and then every man for himself. No grace, no warning, no starting-gun; but the first to finish what he'd had on his plate could claim what was left in the pot. Mother's swooping spoon was breathlessly watched – let the lentils fall where they may. But starving Jack had worked it all out, he followed the spoon with his plate. Absentmindedly Mother would give him first dollop, and very often a second, and as soon as he got it he swallowed it whole, not using his teeth at all. 'More please, I've finished' – the bare plate proved it, so he got the pot-scrapings too. Many the race I've lost to him thus, being just that second slower. But it left me marked with an ugly scar, a twisted, food-crazed nature, so that still I am calling for whole rice puddings and big pots of stew in the night.

THE DAY WAS over and we had used it, running errands or prowling the fields. When evening came we returned to the kitchen, back to its smoky comfort, in from the rapidly cooling air to its wrappings of warmth and cooking. We boys came first, scuffling down the bank, singly, like homing crows. Long tongues of shadows licked the curves of the fields and the trees turned plump and still. I had been off to Painswick to pay the rates, running fast through the long wet grass, and now I was back, panting hard, the job finished, with hay seeds stuck to my legs. A plate of blue smoke hung above our chimney, flat in the motionless air, and every stone in the path as I ran down home shook my bones with arriving joy.

We chopped wood for the night and carried it in; dry beech sticks as brittle as candy. The baker came down with a basket of bread slung carelessly over his shoulder. Eight quartern loaves, cottage-size, black-crusted, were handed in at the door. A few crisp flakes of pungent crust still clung to his empty basket, so we scooped them up on our spit-wet fingers and laid them upon our tongues. The

twilight gathered, the baker shouted goodnight, and whistled his way up the bank. Up in the road his black horse
waited, the cart lamps smoking red.

Indoors, our Mother was cooking pancakes, her face
aglow from the fire. There was a smell of sharp lemon and
salty batter, and a burning hiss of oil. The kitchen was dark
and convulsive with shadows, no lights had yet been lit.
Flames leapt, subsided, corners woke and died, fires
burned in a thousand brasses.

'Poke around for the matches, dear boy,' said Mother.
'Damn me if I know where they got to.'

We lit the candles and set them about, each in its proper
order: two on the mantelpiece, one on the piano, and one
on a plate in the window. Each candle suspended a ball of
light, a luminous fragile glow, which swelled and con-
tracted to the spluttering wick or leaned to the moving air.
Their flames pushed weakly against the red of the fire, too
tenuous to make much headway, revealing our faces more
by casts of darkness than by any clear light they threw.

Next we filled and lit the tall iron lamp and placed it on
the table. When the wick had warmed and was drawing
properly, we turned it up full strength. The flame in the
funnel then sprang alive and rose like a pointed flower,
began to sing and shudder and grow more radiant, throw-
ing pools of light on the ceiling. Even so, the kitchen
remained mostly in shadow, its walls a voluptuous gloom.

The time had come for my violin practice. I began
twanging the strings with relish. Mother was still frying

and rolling up pancakes; my brothers lowered their heads and sighed. I propped my music on the mantelpiece and sliced through a Russian Dance while sweet smells of resin mixed with lemon and fat as the dust flew in clouds from my bow. Now and then I got a note just right, and then Mother would throw me a glance. A glance of piercing, anxious encouragement as she side-stepped my swinging arm. Plump in her slippers, one hand to her cheek, her pan beating time in the other, her hair falling down about her ears, mouth working to help out the tune – old and tired though she was, her eyes were a girl's, and it was for looks such as these that I played.

'Splendid!' she cried. 'Top-hole! Clap-clap! Now give us another, me lad.'

So I slashed away at 'William Tell', and when I did that, plates jumped; and Mother skipped gaily around the hearthrug, and even Tony rocked a bit in his chair.

Meanwhile Jack had cleared some boots from the table, and started his inscrutable homework. Tony, in his corner, began to talk to the cat and play with some fragments of cloth. So with the curtains drawn close and the pancakes coming, we settled down to the evening. When the kettle boiled and the toast was made, we gathered and had our tea. We grabbed and dodged and passed and snatched, and packed our mouths like pelicans.

Mother ate always standing up, tearing crusts off the loaf with her fingers, a hand-to-mouth feeding that expressed her vigilance, like that of a wireless-operator at sea. For most of Mother's attention was fixed on the grate, whose fire must never go out. When it threatened to do so she became seized with hysteria, wailing and wringing her hands, pouring on oil and chopping up chairs in a frenzy to keep it alive. In fact it seldom went out completely, though it was very often ill. But Mother nursed it with skill, banking it up every night and blowing hard on the bars every morning. The state of our fire became as important to us as it must have been to a primitive tribe. When it sulked and sank we were filled with dismay; when it blazed all was well with the world; but if – God save us – it went out altogether, then we were clutched by primeval chills. Then it seemed that the very sun had died, that winter had come for ever, that the wolves of the wilderness were gathering near, and that there was no more hope to look for . . .

But tonight the firelight snapped and crackled, and Mother was in full control. She ruled the range and all its equipment with a tireless, nervous touch. Eating with one hand, she threw on wood with the other, raked the ashes, and heated the oven, put on a kettle, stirred the pot, and spread out some more shirts on the guard. As soon as we boys had finished our tea, we pushed all the crockery aside, piled it up roughly at the far end of the table, and settled down under the lamp. Its light was warm and live around us, a kind of puddle of fire of its own. I set up my book and began to draw. Jack worked at his notes and figures. Tony was playing with some cotton reels, pushing them slowly round the table.

All was silent except Tony's voice, softly muttering his cotton reel story.

'. . . So they come out of this big hole see, and the big chap say Fie and said we'll kill 'em see, and the pirates was waiting up 'ere, and they had this gurt cannon and they went bang fire and the big chap fell down wheeee! and rolled back in the 'ole and I said we got 'em and I run up the 'ill and this boat see was comin' and I jumped on board woosh cruump and I said now I'm captain see and they said fie and I took me 'atchet 'ack 'ack and they all fell plop in the sea wallop and I sailed the boat round 'ere and round 'ere and up 'ere and round 'ere and down 'ere and up 'ere and round 'ere and down 'ere . . .'

OUR HOUSE WAS seventeenth-century Cotswold, and was handsome as they go. It was built of stone, had hand-carved windows, golden surfaces, moss-flaked tiles, and walls so thick they kept a damp chill inside them whatever the season or weather. Its attics and passages were full of walled-up doors which our fingers longed to open – doors that led to certain echoing chambers now sealed off from us for ever. The place had once been a small country manor, and later a public beerhouse; but it had decayed even further by the time we got to it, and was now three poor cottages in one. The house was shaped like a T, and we lived in the down-stroke. The top-stroke – which bore into the side of the bank like a rusty expended shell – was divided separately among two old ladies, one's portion lying above the other's.

Granny Trill and Granny Wallon were rival ancients and lived on each other's nerves, and their perpetual enmity was like mice in the walls and absorbed much of my early days. With their sickle-bent bodies, pale pink eyes, and wild wisps of hedgerow hair, they looked to me the very images of witches and they were also much alike. In all their time as such close neighbours they never exchanged a word. They communicated instead by means of boots and brooms – jumping on floors and knocking on ceilings. They referred to each other as ''Er-Down-Under' and ''Er-Up-Atop, the Varmint'; for each to the other was an airy nothing, a local habitation not fit to be named.

'Er-Down-Under, who lived on our level, was perhaps the smaller of the two, a tiny white shrew who came nibbling through her garden, who clawed squeaking with gossip at our kitchen window, or sat sucking bread in the sun; always mysterious and self-contained and feather-soft in her movements. She had two names, which she changed at will according to the mood of her day. Granny Wallon was her best, and stemmed, we were told, from some distinguished alliance of the past. Behind this crisp and trotting body were certainly rumours of noble blood. But she never spoke of them herself. She was known to have raised a score of children. And she was known to be very poor. She lived on cabbage, bread, and potatoes – but she also made excellent wines.

Granny Wallon's wines were famous in the village, and she spent a large part of her year preparing them. The gathering of the ingredients was the first of the mysteries. At the beginning of April she would go off with her baskets and work round the fields and hedges, and every fine day till the end of summer would find her somewhere out in the valley. One saw her come hobbling home in the evening, bearing her cargoes of crusted flowers, till she had buckets of cowslips, dandelions, elder-blossom crammed into every corner of the house. The elder-flower, drying on her kitchen floor, seemed to cover it with a rancid carpet, a crumbling rime of grey-green blossom fading fast in a dust of summer. Later the tiny grape-cluster of the elder-berry itself would be seething in purple vats, with daisies and orchids thrown in to join it, even strands of the dog-rose bush.

What seasons fermented in Granny Wallon's kitchen, what summers were brought to the boil, with limp flower-heads piled around the floor holding fast to their clotted juices – the sharp spiced honey of those cowslips first, then the coppery reeking dandelion, the bitter poppy's whiff of powder, the cat's-breath, death-green elder. Gleanings of days and a dozen pastures, strippings of lanes and hedges – she bore them home to her flag-tiled kitchen, sorted them each from each, built up her fires and loaded her pots, and added her sugar and yeast. The vats boiled daily in suds of sugar, revolving petals in throbbing water, while the air, aromatic, steamy, embalmed, distilled the hot dews and flowery soups and ran the wine down the dripping walls.

And not only flower-heads went into these brews; the old lady used parsnips, too, potatoes, sloes, crab-apples, quinces, in fact anything she could lay her hands on.

What seasons fermented in Granny Wallon's kitchen, what summers were brought to the boil

Granny Wallon made wine as though demented, out of anything at all; and no doubt, if given enough sugar and yeast, could have made a drink out of a box of old matches.

She never hurried or hoarded her wines, but led them gently through their natural stages. After the boiling they were allowed to settle and to work in the cool of the vats. For several months, using pieces of toast, she scooped off their yeasty sediments. Then she bottled and labelled each liquor in turn and put them away for a year.

At last one was ready, then came the day of distribution. A squeak and a rattle would shake our window, and we'd see the old lady, wispily grinning, waving a large white jug in her hand.

'Hey there, missus! Try this'n, then. It's the first of my last year's cowslip.'

Through the kitchen window she'd fill up our cups and watch us, head cocked, while we drank. The wine in the cups was still and golden, transparent as a pale spring morning. It smelt of ripe grass in some far-away field and its taste was as delicate as air. It seemed so innocent, we would swig away happily and even the youngest guzzled it down. Then a curious rocking would seize the head; tides rose from our feet like a fever, the kitchen walls began to shudder and shift, and we all fell in love with each other.

Very soon we'd be wedged, tight-crammed, in the window, waving our cups for more, while our Mother, bright-eyed, would be mumbling gaily:

'Lord bless you, Granny. Fancy cowsnips and parsney. You must give me the receipt, my dear.'

Granny Wallon would empty the jug in our cups, shake out the last drops on the flowers, then trot off tittering down the garden path, leaving us hugging ourselves in the window.

THE SEASONS OF my childhood seemed (of course) so violent, so intense and true to their nature, that they have become for me ever since a reference of perfection whenever such names are mentioned. They possessed us so completely they seemed to change our nationality; and when I look back to the valley it cannot be one place I see, but village-winter or village-summer, both separate. It becomes increasingly easy in urban life to ignore their extreme humours, but in those days winter and summer dominated our every action, broke into our houses, conscripted our thoughts, ruled our games, and ordered our lives.

Winter was no more typical of our valley than summer, it was not even summer's opposite; it was merely that other place. And somehow one never remembered the journey towards it; one arrived, and winter was here. The day came suddenly when all details were different and the village had to be rediscovered. One's nose went dead so that it hurt to breathe, and there were jigsaws of frost on the

Winter and summer dominated our every action, broke into our houses, conscripted our thoughts, ruled our games, and ordered our lives

window. The light filled the house with a green polar glow; while outside – in the invisible world – there was a strange hard silence, or a metallic creaking, a faint throbbing of twigs and wires.

SUMMER, JUNE SUMMER, with the green back on earth and the whole world unlocked and seething – like winter, it came suddenly and one knew it in bed, almost before waking up; with cuckoos and pigeons hollowing the woods since day-light and the chipping of tits in the pear-blossom.

On the bedroom ceiling, seen first through sleep, was a pool of expanding sunlight – the lake's reflection thrown up through the trees by the rapidly climbing sun. Still drowsy, I watched on the ceiling above me its glittering image reversed, saw every motion of its somnambulant waves and projections of the life upon it. Arrows ran across it from time to time, followed by the far call of a moorhen; I saw ripples of light around each root of the bulrushes, every detail of the lake seemed there. Then suddenly the whole picture would break into pieces, would be smashed like a molten mirror and run amok in tiny globules of gold, frantic and shivering; and I would hear the great slapping of wings on water, building up a steady crescendo, while across the ceiling passed the shadows of swans taking off into the heavy morning. I would hear their cries pass over the house and watch the chaos of light above me, till it slowly settled and re-collected its stars and resumed the lake's still image.

Watching swans take off from my bedroom ceiling was a regular summer wakening. So I woke and looked out through the open window to a morning of cows and cockerels. The beech trees framing the lake and valley seemed to call for a Royal Hunt; but they served equally well for climbing into, and even in June you could still eat their leaves, a tight-folded salad of juices.

Outdoors, one scarcely knew what had happened or remembered any other time. There had never been rain, or frost, or cloud; it had always been like this. The heat from the ground climbed up one's legs and smote one under the chin. The garden, dizzy with scent and bees, burned all over with hot white flowers, each one so blinding an incandescence that it hurt the eyes to look at them.

The villagers took summer like a kind of punishment. The women never got used to it. Buckets of water were being sluiced down paths, the dust was being laid with grumbles, blankets and mattresses hung like tongues from the windows, panting dogs crouched under the rain-tubs. A man went by and asked 'Hot enough for 'ee?' and was answered by a worn-out shriek.

In the builder's stable, well out of the sun, we helped to groom Brown's horse. We smelt the burning of his coat, the horn of his hooves, his hot leather harness, and dung. We fed him on bran, dry as a desert wind, till both we and the horse half-choked. Mr Brown and his family were going for a drive, so we wheeled the trap into the road, backed the blinkered horse between the shafts, and buckled his jingling straps. The road lay deserted in its layer of dust and not a thing seemed to move in the valley. Mr Brown and his best-dressed wife and daughter, followed by his bowler-hatted son-in-law, climbed one by one into the high sprung trap and sat there with ritual stiffness.

'Where we goin' then, Father?'

'Up the hill, for some air.'

'Up the hill? He'll drop down dead.'

'Bide quiet,' said Mr Brown, already dripping with sweat, 'Another word, and you'll go back 'ome.'

He jerked the reins and gave a flick of the whip and the horse broke into a saunter. The women clutched their hats at the unexpected movement, and we watched them till they were out of sight.

When they were gone there was nothing else to look at, the village slipped back into silence. The untarred road wound away up the valley, innocent as yet of motor-cars, wound empty away to other villages, which lay empty too, the hot day long, waiting for the sight of a stranger.

We sat by the roadside and scooped the dust with our hands and made little piles in the gutters. Then we slid through the grass and lay on our backs and just stared at the empty sky. There was nothing to do. Nothing moved or happened, nothing happened at all except summer. Small heated winds blew over our faces, dandelion seeds floated by, burnt sap and roast nettles tingled our nostrils together with the dull rust smell of dry ground. The grass was June high and had come up with a rush, a massed entanglement of species, crested with flowers and spears of wild wheat, and coiled with clambering vetches, the whole of it humming with blundering bees and flickering with scarlet butterflies. Chewing grass on our backs, the grass scaffolding the sky, the summer was all we heard; cuckoos crossed distances on chains of cries, flies buzzed and choked in the ears, and the saw-toothed chatter of mowing-machines drifted on waves of air from the fields.

We moved. We went to the shop and bought sherbet and sucked it through sticks of liquorice. Sucked gently, the sherbet merely dusted the tongue; too hard, and you choked with sweet powders; or if you blew back through the tube the sherbet-bag burst and you disappeared in a blizzard of sugar. Sucking and blowing, coughing and weeping, we scuffled our way down the lane. We drank at the spring to clean our mouths, then threw water at each other and made rainbows. Mr Jones's pond was bubbling with life, and covered with great white lilies – they poured from their leaves like candle-fat, ran molten, then cooled on the water. Moorhens plopped, and dabchicks scooted, insects rowed and skated. New-hatched frogs hopped about like flies, lizards gulped in the grass. The lane itself was crusted with cow-dung, hard baked and smelling good.

We met Sixpence Robinson among the bulrushes, and he said, 'Come and have some fun.' He lived along the lane just past the sheepwash in a farm cottage near a bog. There were five in his family, two girls and three boys, and their names all began with S. There was Sis and Sloppy, Stosher and Sammy, and our good friend Sixpence the Tanner. Sis and Sloppy were both beautiful girls and used to hide from us boys in the gooseberries. It was the brothers we played with: and Sammy, though a cripple, was one of the most agile lads in the village.

Theirs was a good place to be at any time, and they were good to be with. (Like us, they had no father; unlike ours, he was dead.) So today, in the spicy heat of their bog, we sat round on logs and whistled, peeled sticks, played mouth-organs, dammed up the stream, and cut harbours in the cool clay banks. Then we took all the pigeons out of their dovecots and ducked them in the water-butt, held them under till their beaks started bubbling then threw them up in the air. Splashing spray from their wings they flew round the house, then came back to roost like fools. (Sixpence had a one-eyed pigeon called Spike who he boasted could stay under longest, but one day the poor bird, having broken all records, crashed for ever among the cabbages.)

When all this was over, we retired to the paddock and played cricket under the trees. Sammy, in his leg-irons, charged up and down. Hens and guinea-fowl took to the trees. Sammy hopped and bowled like murder at us, and we defended our stumps with our lives. The cracked bat clouting; the cries in the reeds; the smells of fowls and water; the long afternoon with the steep hills around us watched by Sloppy still hid in the gooseberries – it seemed down here that no disasters could happen, that nothing could ever touch us. This was Sammy's and Sixpence's; the place past the sheepwash, the hide-out unspoiled by authority, where drowned pigeons flew and cripples ran free; where it was summer, in some ways, always.

SUMMER WAS ALSO the time of these: of sudden plenty, of slow hours and actions, of diamond haze and dust on the eyes, of the valley in post-vernal slumber; of burying birds out of seething corruption; of Mother sleeping heavily at noon; of jazzing wasps and dragonflies, haystooks and thistle-seeds, snows of white butterflies, skylarks' eggs, bee-orchids, and frantic ants; of wolf-cub parades, and boy scouts' bugles; of sweat running down the legs; of boiling potatoes on bramble fires, of flames glass-blue in the sun; of lying naked in the hill-cold stream; begging pennies for bottles of pop; of girls' bare arms and unripe cherries, green apples and liquid walnuts; of fights and falls and new-scabbed knees, sobbing pursuits and flights; of pic-nics high up in the crumbling quarries, of butter running like oil, of sunstroke, fever, and cucumber peel stuck cool to one's burning brow. All this, and the feeling that it would never end, that such days had come for ever, with the pump drying up and the water-butt crawling, and the chalk ground hard as the moon. All sights twice-brilliant and smells twice-sharp, all game-days twice as long. Dou-ble charged as we were, like the meadow ants, with the frenzy of the sun, we used up the light to its last violet drop, and even then couldn't go to bed.

We used up the light to its last violet drop, and even then we couldn't go to bed

When darkness fell, and the huge moon rose, we stirred to a second life. Then boys went calling along the roads, wild slit-eyed animal calls, Walt Kerry's naked nasal yodel, Boney's jackal scream. As soon as we heard them we crept outdoors, out of our stifling bedrooms, stepped out into moonlight warm as the sun to join our chalk-white, moon-masked gang.

Games in the moon. Games of pursuit and capture. Games that the night demanded. Best of all, Fox and Hounds – go where you like, and the whole of the valley to hunt through. Two chosen boys loped away through the trees and were immediately swallowed in shadow. We gave them five minutes, then set off after them. They had churchyard, farmyard, barns, quarries, hilltops, and woods to run to. They had all night, and the whole of the moon, and five miles of country to hide in . . .

Padding softly, we ran under the melting stars, through sharp garlic woods, through blue blazed fields, following the scent by the game's one rule, the question and answer cry. Every so often, panting for breath, we paused to check on our quarry. Bullet heads lifted, teeth shone in the moon. 'Whistle-or-'OLLER! Or-we-shall-not-FOLLER!' It was a cry on two notes, prolonged. From the other side of the hill, above white fields of mist, the faint fox-cry came back. We were off again then, through the waking night, among sleepless owls and badgers, while our quarry slipped off into another parish and would not be found for hours.

Round about midnight we ran them to earth, exhausted

under a haystack. Until then we had chased them through all the world, through jungles, swamps, and tundras, across pampas plains and steppes of wheat and plateaux of shooting stars, while hares made love in the silver grasses, and the large hot moon climbed over us, raising tides in my head of night and summer that move there even yet.

THE YEAR REVOLVED around the village, the festivals round the year, the church round the festivals, the Squire round the church, and the village round the Squire. The Squire was our centre, a crumbling moot tree; and few indeed of our local celebrations could take place without his shade. On the greater occasions he let us loose in his gardens, on the smaller gave us buns and speeches; and at historic moments of national rejoicing – when kings were born, enemies vanquished, or the Conservatives won an election – he ransacked his boxrooms for fancy-dresses that we might rejoice in a proper manner.

The first big festival that I can remember was Peace Day in 1919. It was a day of magical transformations, of tears and dusty sunlight, of bands, processions, and buns by the cartload; and I was so young I thought it normal . . .

We had all been provided with fancy-dress, and that seemed normal too. Apart from the Squire's contribution Marjorie had been busy for weeks stitching up glories for

ourselves and the neighbours. No makeshift, rag-bag cob-
bling either; Marjorie had worked as though for a
wedding.

On the morning of the feast Poppy Green came to the
house to try on her angel's dress. She was five years old and
about my size. She had russet curls like apple peelings, a
polished pumpkin face, a fruity air of exploding puddings,
and a perpetual cheeky squint. I loved her, she was like a
portable sweet-shop. This morning I watched my sisters
dress her. She was supposed to represent a spirit. They'd
made her a short frilly frock, a tinfoil helmet, cardboard
wings, and a wand with a star. When they'd clothed her
they stood her up on the mantelpiece and had a good look
at her. Then they went off awhile on some other business
and left us alone together.

'Fly!' I commanded. 'You got wings, ain't you?'

Poppy squirmed and wiggled her shoulders.

I grew impatient and pushed her off the mantelpiece,
and she fell with a howl into the fireplace. Looking down
at her, smudged with coal and tears, her wand and wings
all crumpled, I felt nothing but rage and astonishment. She
should have been fluttering round the room.

They sponged and soothed her, and Poppy trotted
home, her bent wand clutched in her hand. Then shapes
and phantoms began to run through the village, and we
started to get ready ourselves. Marge appeared as Queen
Elizabeth, with Phyllis her lady-in-waiting. Marjorie, who
was sixteen and at her most beautiful, wore a gown of

ermine, a brocaded bodice, and a black cap studded with pearls. She filled the kitchen with such a glow of grace that we just stood and gaped at her. It was the first time I had seen Queen Elizabeth, but this was no sharp-faced Tudor. Tender and proud in her majestic robes, she was the Queen of Heaven, risen from the dust, unrecognizable as Marge till she spoke, and her eyes shone down on us from her veils of ermine like emeralds laid in snow. Thirteen-year-old Phyllis, with finery of her own, skipped like a magpie around her, wearing a long chequered dress of black and white velvet, and a hat full of feathers and moths.

The rest of us, whom Marjorie had dressed, were the result of homespun inspirations. Dorothy, as 'Night', was perhaps the most arresting; an apparition of unearthly beauty, a flash of darkness, a strip of nocturnal sky, mysteriously cloaked in veils of black netting entangled with silver paper. A crescent moon lay across her breast, a comet across her brow, and her long dark curls fell in coils of midnight and were sprinkled with tinsel dust. I smelt frost when I saw her and heard a crackling of stars; familiar Dorothy had grown far and disturbing.

Brother Jack had refused to be dressed up at all, unless in some aspect of recognized valour. So they hung him in green, gave him a bow and arrow, and he called himself Robin Hood. Little Tony was dressed as a market-girl, curly-headed and pretty as love, bare-armed and bonneted, carrying a basket of flowers, but so proud we forgave him his frock.

As for me, a squat neck and solid carriage made the part I should play inevitable. I was John Bull – whoever he was – but I quickly surmised his importance. I remember the girls stuffing me into my clothes with many odd squeals and giggles. Gravely I offered an arm or leg, but remained dignified and aloof. Marjorie had assembled the ritual garments with her usual flair and cunning. I wore a top-hat and choker, a union-jack waistcoat, a frock-coat, and pillowcase breeches. But I'd been finished off hurriedly with gaiters of cardboard fastened loosely together with pins – a slovenly makeshift which offended my taste, and which I was never able to forgive.

This Peace Day I remember as a blur of colour, leading from fury to triumph. There was a procession with a band. I walked alone solemnly. Fantastic disguises surrounded me; every single person seemed covered with beards, false-noses, bootblack, and wigs. We had not marched far when my boots fell off, followed by my cardboard gaiters. As I stopped to find them, the procession swept over me. I sat down by the roadside and howled. I howled because I could hear the band disappearing, because I was John Bull and it should not have happened. I was picked up by a carriage, restored to the procession, then placed on a trolley and pulled. Cross-legged on the trolley, bare-footed and gaiterless, I rode like a prince through the village.

Dusty, sweating from its long route-march, the procession snaked round the houses. The old and infirm stood and cheered from the gutters; I nodded back from my trolley. At last we entered the cool beech wood through which the Squire's drive twisted. The brass-band's thunder bounced back from the boughs. Owls hooted and flapped away.

We came out of the wood into the Big House gardens, and the sun returned in strength. Doves and pigeons flew out of the cedars. The swans took off from the lake. On the steps of the Manor stood the wet-eyed Squire, already in tears at the sight of us. His mother, in a speech from a basket-chair, mentioned the glory of God, the Empire, us; and said we wasn't to touch the flowers.

With the procession dispersed, I was tipped off the trolley, and I wandered away through the grounds. Flags and roses moved against the sky, bright figures among the bushes. Japanese girls and soot-faced savages grew strangely from banks of lilac. I saw Charlie Chaplin, Peter the Pieman, a collection of upright tigers, a wounded soldier about my age, and a bride on the arm of a monkey.

Later I was given a prize by the Squire and was photographed in a group by a rockery. I still have that picture, all sepia shadows, a leaf ripped from that summer day. Surrounded by girls in butter muslin, by druids and eastern kings, I am a figure rooted in unshakeable confidence, oval, substantial, and proud. About two feet high and two feet broad, my breeches like slack balloons, I stand, top-hatted, with a tilted face as severe as on a Roman coin. Others I recognize are gathered round me, all marked by that day's white dust. Tony has lost his basket of flowers, Jack his bow and arrow. Poppy Green has had her wings torn off

and is grasping a broken lily. She stands beside me, squint-
ing fiercely, ruffled a bit by the heat, and the silver letters
across her helmet – which I couldn't read then – say PEACE.

OUR VILLAGE OUTINGS were both sacred and secular, and
were also far between. One seldom, in those days, strayed
beyond the parish boundaries, except for the annual Choir
Outing. In the meantime we had our own tribal wander-
ings, unsanctified though they were, when a sudden fine
morning would send us forth in families for a day's nutting
or blackberrying. So up we'd go to the wilder end of the
valley, to the bramble-entangled Scrubs, bearing baskets
and buckets and flasks of cold tea, like a file of foraging
Indians. Blackberries clustered against the sky, heavy and
dark as thunder, which we plucked and gobbled, hour after
hour, lips purple, hands stained to the wrists. Or later,
mushrooms, appearing like manna, buttoning the shaggy
grass, found in the mists of September mornings with the
wet threads of spiders on them. They came in the night
from nowhere, rootless, like a scattering of rubber balls.
Their suckers clung to the roots of grass and broke off with
a rubbery snap. The skin rubbed away like the bark of a
birch tree, the flesh tasted of something unknown . . . At
other times there would be wild green damsons, tiny
plums, black sloes, pink crab-apples – the free waste of the
woods, an unpoliced bounty, which we'd carry back home
in bucketfuls. Whether we used them for jam or jellies or
pies, or just left them to rot, didn't matter.

Then sometimes there'd be a whole day's outing, perhaps to Sheepscombe to visit relations – a four-mile walk, which to our short legs seemed further, so that we needed all day to do it. We would start out early, with the sun just rising and the valley wrapped in mist . . .

'It's going to be hot,' says our Mother brightly, and usually she is right. We climb up slowly towards Bulls Cross, picking at the bushes for birds'-nests. Or we stop to dig holes or to swing on gates while Mother looks back at the view. 'What a picture,' she murmurs. 'Green as green . . . And those poppies, red as red.' The mist drags the tree-tops, flies away in the sky, and there is suddenly blue air all round us.

Painswick sprawls white in the other valley, like the skeleton of a foundered mammoth. But active sounds of its working morning – carts and buzz-saws, shouts and hammering – come drifting in gusts towards us. The narrow lane that leads to Sheepscombe bends steeply away on our right. 'Step out, young men!' our Mother says crisply. She begins to teach us a hymn; the kind that cries for some lost land of paradise, and goes well with a tambourine. I've not heard it before (nor ever since), but it entirely enshrines our outing – the remote, shaggy valley in which we find ourselves, the smell of hot straw on the air, dog-roses and distances, dust and spring waters, and the long day's journey, by easy stages, to the sheep-folds of our wild relations.

They are waiting for us with warm ginger-beer, and a

dinner of broad beans and bacon. Aunty Fan says, 'Annie, come in out of the sun. You must be ready to drop.' We go indoors and find our Uncle Charlie hacking at the bacon with a bill-hook. Young cousin Edie and her cautious brothers seem to be pondering whether to punch our heads. Our Gramp comes in from his cottage next door, dressed in mould-green corduroy suiting. We sit down and eat, and the cousins kick us under the table, from excitement rather than spite. Then we play with their ferrets, spit down their well, have a fight, and break down a wall. Later we are called for and given a beating, then we climb up the tree by the earth closet. Edie climbs highest, till we bite her legs, then she hangs upside down and screams. It has been a full, far-flung, and satisfactory day; dusk falls, and we say good-bye.

Back down the lane in the thick hot darkness we walk drowsily, heavy with boots. Night odours come drifting from woods and gardens; sweet musks and sharp green acids. In the sky the fat stars bounce up and down, rhythmically, as we trudge along. Glow-worms, brighter than lamps or candles, spike the fields with their lemon fires, while huge horned beetles stumble out of the dark and buzz blindly around our heads.

Then Painswick appears – a starfish of light dilating in a pool of distance. We hurry across the haunted common and come at last to the top of our valley. The village waterfall, still a mile away, lifts its cool, familiar murmur. We are nearing home, we are almost there: Mother starts to recite a poem. 'I remember, I remember, the house where I was born . . .' She says it right through, and I tag beside her watching the trees walk past in the sky . . .

THE FIRST CHOIR OUTING we ever had was a jaunt in a farm-wagon to Gloucester. Only the tenors and basses and the treble boys were included in that particular treat. Later, with the coming of the horse-brake and charabanc, the whole village took part as well. With the help of the powerful new charabanc we even got out of the district altogether, rattling away to the ends of the earth, to Bristol or even further.

One year the Outing was to Weston-super-Mare, and we had saved up for months to be worthy of it. We spent the night before preparing our linen, and the girls got up at dawn to make sandwiches. The first thing I did when I came down that morning was to go out and look at the weather. The sky was black, and Tony was behind the lavatory praying hard through his folded hands. When he saw that I'd seen him he began to scratch and whistle, but the whole thing was a very bad sign.

We couldn't eat breakfast, the porridge was like gravel; so Jack and I ran up the bank to see what was going on. Families were already gathering for the charabancs, so we ran back down again. The girls were ready, and Tony was ready. Mother was raking under the piano with a broom-stick.

'Come on, our Mother! They'll go without us!'

'I've just got to find my corsets.'

She found them; then started very slowly to wash, like a duck with all summer to do it. We stood round and nagged her, rigid with nerves.

'Run along – you're under my feet.'

So we left her, and scampered along to the Woolpack. The whole village was waiting by now; mothers with pig-buckets stuffed with picnics, children with cocoa-tin spades, fathers with bulging overcoats lined entirely with clinking bottles. There was little Mrs Tulley collecting the fares and plucking at her nervous cheeks; Mr Vick, the shopkeeper, carrying his keys in a basket; the two dress-makers in unclaimed gowns; and Lily Nelson, a fugitive from her brother, whispering, 'You mustn't tell Arnold – he'd kill me.' The Squire's old gardener had brought a basket of pigeons which he planned to release from the pier. And the postman, having nobody to deliver his letters to, had dumped them, and was coming along too.

Faces looked pale in the early light. Men sniffed and peered at the sky. 'Don't look too good, do it?' 'Can't say it do.' 'Bloody black over Stroud.' 'Might clear though . . .' Teeth were sucked in, heads doubtfully shaken; I felt the doom of storm-sickness on me.

The vicar arrived to see us off – his pyjamas peeping out from his raincoat. 'There's a very nice church near the Promenade . . . I trust you will all spare a moment . . .' He issued each choirboy with his shilling for dinner, then dodged back home to bed. The last to turn up was Herbert the gravedigger, with something queer in a sack. The last, that is, except our Mother, of whom there was still no sign.

Then the charabancs arrived and everyone clambered aboard, fighting each other for seats. We abandoned our Mother and climbed aboard too, feeling guilty and miserable. The charabancs were high, with broad open seats and with folded tarpaulins at the rear, upon which, as choirboys, we were privileged to perch and to fall off and break our necks. We all took our places, people wrapped themselves in blankets, horns sounded, and we were ready. 'Is everyone present?' piped the choirmaster. Shamefully, Jack and I kept silent.

Our Mother, as usual, appeared at that moment, a distant trotting figure, calling and waving her handbags gaily to disarm what impatience there might be. 'Come on, Mother Lee! We near went without you!' Beaming, she climbed aboard. 'I just had to wash out my scarf,' she said, and tied it on the windscreen to dry. And there it blew like a streaming pennant as we finally drove out of the village.

In our file of five charabancs, a charioted army, we swept down the thundering hills. At the speed and height of our vehicles the whole valley took on new dimensions; woods rushed beneath us, and fields and flies were devoured in a gulp of air. We were windborne now by motion and pride, we cheered everything, beast and fowl, and taunted with heavy ironical shouts those unfortunates still working in the fields. We kept this up till we had roared through Stroud, then we entered the stranger's country. It was no longer so easy to impress pedestrians that we were the Annual Slad Choir Outing. So we settled down, and opened our sandwiches, and began to criticize the farming we passed through.

The flatness of the Severn Valley now seemed dull after our swooping hills, the salmon-red sandstone of the Clifton Gorges too florid compared with our chalk. Everything began to appear strange and comic, we hooted at the shapes of the hayricks, laughed at the pitiful condition of the cattle – 'He won't last long – just look at 'is knees.' We began to look round fondly at our familiar selves, drawn close by this alien country. Waves of affection and loyalty embraced us. We started shouting across the seats. 'Harry! Hey, Harry! Say whatcher, Harry! Bit of all right, ain't it, you? Hey, Bert! 'Ow's Bert? 'Ow you doin', ole sparrer? Where's Walt? Hey there, Walt! Watcher!'

Mile after rattling mile we went, under the racing sky, flying neckties and paper kites from the back, eyes screwed in the weeping wind. The elders, protected in front by the windscreen, chewed strips of bacon, or slept. Mother pointed out landmarks and lectured the sleepers on points of historical interest. Then a crawling boy found the basket of pigeons and the coach exploded with screams and wings . . .

The weather cleared as we drove into Weston, and we halted on the Promenade. 'The seaside,' they said: we gazed around us, but we saw no sign of the sea. We saw a vast blue sky and an infinity of mud stretching away to the shadows of Wales. But rousing smells of an invisible ocean astonished our land-locked nostrils: salt, and wet weeds, and fishy oozes; a sharp difference in every breath. Our deep-ditched valley had not been prepared for this, for we had never seen such openness, the blue windy world seemed to have blown quite flat, bringing the sky to the level of our eyebrows. Canvas booths flapped on the edge of the Prom, mouths crammed with shellfish and vinegar; there were rows of prim boarding-houses (each the size of our Vicarage); bath-chairs, carriages, and donkeys; and stilted far out on the rippled mud a white pier like a sleeping dragon.

The blue day was ours; we rattled our money and divided up into groups. 'Hey, Jake, Steve; let's go have a wet' – and the men shuffled off down a side street. 'I'm beat after that, Mrs Jones, ain't you? – there's a clean place down by the bandstand.' The old women nodded, and went seeking their comforts; the young ones to stare at the policemen.

Meanwhile, we boys just picked up and ran; we had a world of mud to deal with. The shops and streets ended suddenly, a frontier to the works of man; and beyond – the mud, salt winds, and birds, a kind of double ration of light, a breathless space neither fenced nor claimed, and far out a horizon of water. We whinnied like horses and charged up and down, every hoof-mark written behind us. If you stamped in this mud, you brought it alive, the footprint began to speak, it sucked and sighed and filled with water, became a foot cut out of the sky. I dug my fingers into a stretch of mud to see how deep it was, felt a hard flat pebble and drew it out and examined it in the palm of my hand. Suddenly, it cracked, and put out two claws; I dropped it in horror, and ran . . .

Half the village now had hired themselves chairs and were bravely facing the wind. Mrs Jones was complaining about Weston tea: 'It's made from the drains, I reckon.' The Squire's old gardener, having lost his pigeons, was trying to catch gulls in a basket; and the gravedigger (who appeared to have brought his spade) was out on the mud digging holes. Then the tide came in like a thick red sludge, and we all went on the pier.

Magic construction striding the waves, loaded with freaks and fancies, water-chutes and crumpled mirrors, and a whole series of nightmares for a penny. One glided secretly to one's favourite machine, the hot coin burning one's hand, to command a murder, a drunk's delirium, a haunted grave, or a Newgate hanging. This last, of course, was my favourite; what dread power one's penny purchased – the painted gallows, the nodding priest, the felon with his face of doom. At a touch they jerked through their ghastly dance, the priest, hangman, and the convict, joined together by rods and each one condemned as it were to perpetual torment. Their ritual motions led to the jerk of the corpse; the figures froze and the lights went out. Another penny restored the lights, brought back life to the cataleptic trio, and dragged the poor felon once more to the gallows to be strangled all over again.

That white pier shining upon the waves seemed a festive charnel house. With our mouths hanging open, sucking gory sticks of rock, we groped hungrily from horror to horror. For there were sideshows too, as well as the machines with hair-raising freaks under glass – including a two-headed Indian, a seven-legged sheep, and a girl's eye with a child coiled inside it.

We spent more time on that turgid pier than anywhere else in Weston. Then the tide went out, and evening fell, and we returned to the waiting charabancs. People came wandering from all directions, with bags full of whelks and seaweed, the gravedigger was dragged from his holes in the sand, and our numbers were checked and counted. Then we were all in our seats, the tarpaulin pulled over us, and with a blast of horns we left.

A long homeward drive through the red twilight, through landscapes already relinquished, the engines humming, the small children sleeping, and the young girls gobbling shrimps. At sunset we stopped at a gaslit pub for the men to have one more drink. This lasted till all of them turned bright pink and started embracing their wives. Then we repacked the charabancs, everyone grew drowsy, and we drove through the darkness beyond Bristol. The last home stretch: someone played a harmonica; we boys groped for women to sleep on, and slept, to the sway and sad roar of the coach and the men's thick boozy singing.

We passed Stroud at last and climbed the valley road, whose every curve our bodies recognized, whose every slant we leaned to, though still half asleep, till we woke to the smell of our houses. We were home, met by lanterns – and the Outing was over. With subdued 'Goodnights' we collected into families, then separated towards our beds. Where soon I lay, my head ringing with sleep, my ears full of motors and organs, my shut eyes printed with the images of the day – mud, and red rock, and hangmen . . .

THE DAY ROSIE Burdock decided to take me in hand was a motionless day of summer, creamy, hazy, and amber-coloured, with the beech trees standing in heavy sunlight as though clogged with wild wet honey. It was the time of hay-making, so when we came out of school Jack and I went to the farm to help.

The whirr of the mower met us across the stubble, rabbits jumped like firecrackers about the fields, and the hay smelt crisp and sweet. The farmer's men were all hard at work, raking, turning, and loading. Tall, whiskered fellows forked the grass, their chests like bramble patches. The air swung with their forks and the swathes took wing and rose like eagles to the tops of the wagons. The farmer gave us a short fork each and we both pitched in with the rest . . .

I stumbled on Rosie behind a haycock, and she grinned up at me with the sly, glittering eyes of her mother. She wore her tartan frock and cheap brass necklace, and her bare legs were brown with hay-dust.

'Get out a there,' I said. 'Go on.'

Rosie had grown and was hefty now, and I was terrified of her. In her cat-like eyes and curling mouth I saw unnatural wisdoms more threatening than anything I could imagine. The last time we'd met I'd hit her with a cabbage stump. She bore me no grudge, just grinned.

'I got sommat to show ya.'

'You push off,' I said.

I felt dry and dripping, icy hot. Her eyes glinted, and I stood rooted. Her face was wrapped in a pulsating haze and her body seemed to flicker with lightning.

'You thirsty?' she said.

'I ain't, so there.'

'You be,' she said. 'C'mon.'

So I stuck the fork into the ringing ground and followed her, like doom.

We went a long way, to the bottom of the field, where a wagon stood half-loaded. Festoons of untrimmed grass hung down like curtains all around it. We crawled underneath, between the wheels, into a herb-scented cave of darkness. Rosie scratched about, turned over a sack, and revealed a stone jar of cider.

'It's cider,' she said. 'You ain't to drink it though. Not much of it, any rate.'

Huge and squat, the jar lay on the grass like an unexploded bomb. We lifted it up, unscrewed the stopper, and smelt the whiff of fermented apples. I held the jar to my mouth and rolled my eyes sideways, like a beast at a water-hole. 'Go on,' said Rosie. I took a deep breath . . .

Never to be forgotten, that first long secret drink of golden fire, juice of those valleys and of that time, wine of wild orchards, of russet summer, of plump red apples, and Rosie's burning cheeks. Never to be forgotten, or ever tasted again . . .

I put down the jar with a gulp and a gasp. Then I turned to look at Rosie. She was yellow and dusty with buttercups and seemed to be purring in the gloom; her hair was rich as a wild bee's nest and her eyes were full of stings. I did not know what to do about her, nor did I know what not to do. She looked smooth and precious, a thing of unplumbable mysteries, and perilous as quicksand.

'Rosie . . .' I said, on my knees, and shaking.

She crawled with a rustle of grass towards me, quick and superbly assured. Her hand in mine was like a small wet flame which I could neither hold nor throw away. Then Rosie, with a remorseless, reedy strength, pulled me down from my tottering perch, pulled me down, down into her wide green smile and into the deep subaqueous grass.

Then I remember little, and that little, vaguely. Skin drums beat in my head. Rosie was close-up, salty, an invisible touch, too near to be seen or measured. And it seemed that the wagon under which we lay went floating away like a barge, out over the valley where we rocked unseen, swinging on motionless tides.

Then she took off her boots and stuffed them with

Never to be forgotten, that first long secret drink of golden fire, juice of those valleys and of that time, wine of wild orchards

flowers. She did the same with mine. Her parched voice crackled like flames in my ears. More fires were started. I drank more cider. Rosie told me outrageous fantasies. She liked me, she said, better than Walt, or Ken, Boney Harris, or even the curate. And I admitted to her, in a loud, rough voice, that she was even prettier than Betty Gleed. For a long time we sat with our mouths very close, breathing the same hot air. We kissed, once only, so dry and shy, it was like two leaves colliding in air.

At last the cuckoos stopped singing and slid into the woods. The mowers went home and left us. I heard Jack calling as he went down the lane, calling my name till I heard him no more. And still we lay in our wagon of grass tugging at each other's hands, while her husky, perilous whisper drugged me and the cider beat gongs in my head . . .

Night came at last, and we crawled out from the wagon and stumbled together towards home. Bright dew and glow-worms shone over the grass, and the heat of the day grew softer. I felt like a giant; I swung from the trees and plunged my arms into nettles just to show her. Whatever I did seemed valiant and easy. Rosie carried her boots, and smiled.

There was something about that evening which dilates the memory, even now. The long hills slavered like Chinese dragons, crimson in the setting sun. The shifting lane lassoed my feet and tried to trip me up. And the lake, as we passed it, rose hissing with waves and tried to drown us among its cannibal fish.

Perhaps I fell in – though I don't remember. But here I lost Rosie for good. I found myself wandering home alone, wet through, and possessed by miracles. I discovered extraordinary tricks of sight. I could make trees move and leap-frog each other, and turn bushes into roaring trains. I could lick up the stars like acid drops and fall flat on my face without pain. I felt magnificent, fateful, and for the first time in my life, invulnerable to the perils of night.

When at last I reached home, still dripping wet, I was bursting with power and pleasure. I sat on the chopping-block and sang 'Fierce Raged the Tempest' and several other hymns of that nature. I went on singing till long after supper-time, bawling alone in the dark. Then Harold and Jack came and frog-marched me to bed. I was never the same again . . .

THE LAST DAYS of my childhood were also the last days of the village. I belonged to that generation which saw, by chance, the end of a thousand years' life. The change came late to our Cotswold valley, didn't really show itself till the late 1920s; I was twelve by then, but during that handful of years I witnessed the whole thing happen.

Myself, my family, my generation, were born in a world of silence; a world of hard work and necessary patience, of backs bent to the ground, hands massaging the crops, of waiting on weather and growth; of villages like ships in the empty landscapes and the long walking distances between them; of white narrow roads, rutted by hooves and cart-wheels, innocent of oil or petrol, down which people passed rarely, and almost never for pleasure, and the horse was the fastest thing moving. Man and horse were all the power we had – abetted by levers and pulleys. But the horse was king, and almost everything grew around him: fodder, smithies, stables, paddocks, distances, and the rhythm of our days. His eight miles an hour was the limit of our movements, as it had been since the days of the Romans. That eight miles an hour was life and death, the size of our world, our prison.

This was what we were born to, and all we knew at first. Then, to the scream of the horse, the change began. The brass-lamped motor-car came coughing up the road, followed by the clamorous charabanc; the solid-tyred bus climbed the dusty hills and more people came and went. Chickens and dogs were the early sacrifices, falling demented beneath the wheels. The old folk, too, had strokes and seizures, faced by speeds beyond comprehension. Then scarlet motor-bikes, the size of five-barred gates, began to appear in the village, on which our youths roared like rockets up the two-minute hills, then spent weeks making repairs and adjustments.

These appearances did not immediately alter our lives; the cars were freaks and rarely seen, the motor-bikes mostly in pieces, we used the charabancs only once a year, and our buses at first were experiments. Meanwhile Lew Ayres, wearing a bowler-hat, ran his wagonette to Stroud twice a week. The carriage held six, and the fare was two-pence, but most people preferred to walk. Mr West, from Sheepscombe, ran a cart every day, and would carry your parcels for a penny. But most of us still did the journey on foot, heads down to the wet Welsh winds, ignoring the carters – whom we thought extortionate – and spending a long hard day at our shopping.

But the car-shying horses with their rolling eyes gave signs of the hysteria to come. Soon the village would break, dissolve, and scatter, become no more than a place for pensioners. It had a few years left, the last of its thousand, and they passed almost without our knowing. They passed quickly, painlessly, in motor-bike jaunts, in the shadows of the new picture-palace, in quick trips to Gloucester (once a foreign city) to gape at the jazzy shops. Yet right to the end, like the false strength that precedes death, the old life seemed as lusty as ever.

The church, for instance, had never appeared more powerful. Its confident bell rang out each Sunday; the village heard it, asked no questions, put on satin and serge, filed into the pews, bobbed and nodded, frowned at its children, crouched and prayed, bawled or quavered through hymns, and sat in blank rows or jerkily slept while the curate reeled off those literary sermons which he had hired from the ecclesiastical library.

Sunday, far from being a day of rest, was in some ways tougher than a weekday; it was never torpid and it gave one a lift, being a combination of both indulgence and discipline. On that one day in seven – having bathed the night before – we were clean, wore our best, and ate meat. The discipline was Sunday School, learning the Collect, and worship both morning and evening. Neither mood nor inclination had any say in the matter, nor had doubt occurred to us yet.

Sunday mornings at home were the usual rush – chaos

in the kitchen, shrill orders to wash, and everyone's eyes on the clock. We polished our hair with grease and water, and scrubbed ourselves under the pump. Being Sunday, there was a pound of large sausages for breakfast, fried black and bursting with fat. One dipped them in pepper and ate them in haste, an open prayer-book propped up by the plate.

'Heavens alive, you'll be late, our lad.'

Gobble, mumble, and choke.

'What *are* you up to? Get a move on do.'

'Leave off – I'm learning the Collect.'

'What's that you say?'

'I-Gotta-Learn-Me-Collect!'

'Hurry up and learn it then.'

'I can't hurry up! Not if you keep on! . . .'

But it was really not difficult at all; ten inscrutable lines absorbed between mouthfuls, and usually on the run. Up the bank, down the road, the greasy prayer-book in one hand, the remains of the sausage in the other: 'Almighty and Most Merciful Father, who alone worketh Great Marvels . . .' In five minutes it was all in my head.

At Sunday School Miss Bagnall, polishing her nose, said: 'The Collect – now who will oblige . . .' I would jump to my feet and gabble, word perfect, the half page of sonorous syllables. It came in through the eyes and out through the mouth, and left no trace of its passing. Except that I can never read a Collect today without tasting a crisp burnt sausage . . .

After an hour of Sunday School we all went to the church, the choir going straight to the vestry. Here we huddled ourselves into our grimy robes, which only got washed at Easter. The parson lined us up and gave us a short, sharp prayer; then we filed into the stalls, took our privileged places, and studied the congregation. The Sunday School infants packed the bleak north wing, heads fuzzy as frosted flowers. The rest of the church was black with adults, solemn in cat's-fur and feathers. Most were arranged in family groups, but here and there a young couple, newly engaged, sat red in the neck and hands. The leading benches contained our gentry, their pews marked with visiting cards: the Lords of the Manor, Squire Jones and the Croomes; then the Army, the Carvossos and Dovetons; the rich and settled spinsters, the Misses Abels and Bagnalls; and finally the wealthier farmers. All were neatly arranged by protocol, with the Squire up front by the pulpit. Through prayers and psalms and rackety hymns he slept like a beaming child, save when a visiting preacher took some rhetorical flight, when he'd wake with a loud, 'God damn!'

Morning service began with an organ voluntary, perhaps a Strauss waltz played very slow. The organ was old, and its creaks and sighs were often louder than the music itself. The organ was blown by an ordinary pump-handle which made the process equally rowdy; and Rex Brown, the blower, hidden away in his box – and only visible to us in the choir – enlivened the service by parodying it in mime or by carving girls' names on the woodwork.

But in the packed congregation solemnity ruled. There was power, lamentation, full-throated singing, heavy prayers, and public repentance. No one in the village stayed away without reason, and no one yet wished to do so. We had come to the church because it was Sunday, just as we washed our clothes on Monday. There was also God taking terrible notes – a kind of Squire-archical rent-collector, ever ready to record the tenants' backsliding and to evict them if their dues weren't paid.

This morning service was also something else. It was a return to the Ark of all our species in the face of the ever-threatening flood. We are free of that need now and when the flood does come shall drown proud and alone, no doubt. As it was, the lion knelt down with the lamb, the dove perched on the neck of the hawk, sheep nuzzled wolf, we drew warmth from each other and knew ourselves beasts of one kingdom . . .

That was Sunday morning. With the service over, there was gossip among the gravestones, a slow walk home to roasted dinners, then a nap with the *News of the World*. The elders dozed sexily through the fat afternoon, while the young went again to Sunday School. Later came Even-song, which was as different from Matins as a tryst from a Trafalgar Square rally. The atmosphere was gentler, moonier, more private; the service was considered to be voluntary. We choirboys, of course, were compelled to go, but for the rest they went who would.

The church at night, in the dark of the churchyard, was

just a strip of red-fired windows. Inside, the oil-lamps and motionless candles narrowed the place with shadows. The display of the morning was absent now; the nave was intimate, and sleepy. Only a few solitary worshippers were present this time, each cloaked in a separate absorption: a Miss Bagnall, Widow White, the church-cleaning woman, a widower, and the postman at the back. The service was almost a reverie, our hymns nocturnal and quiet, the psalms traditional and never varying so that one could sing them without a book. The scattered faithful, half-obscured by darkness, sang them as though to themselves. 'Lord, now lettest Thou Thy servant depart in peace . . .' It was sung, eyes closed, in trembling tones. It could not have been sung in the morning.

From our seats in the choir we watched the year turn: Christmas, Easter and Whitsun, Rogation Sunday and prayers for rain, the Church following the plough very close. Harvest Festival perhaps was the one we liked best, the one that came nearest home. Then how heavily and abundantly was our small church loaded; the cream of the valley was used to decorate it. Everyone brought of his best from field and garden; and to enter the church on Harvest morning was like crawling head first into a horn of plenty, a bursting granary, a vegetable stall, a grotto of bright flowers. The normally bare walls sprouted leaves and fruits, the altar great stooks of wheat, and ornamental loaves as big as cartwheels stood parked by the communion rails. Bunches of grapes, from the Squire's own vines, hung blue from the lips of the pulpit. Gigantic and useless marrows abounded, leeks and onions festooned the pews, there were eggs and butter on the lectern shelves, the windows were heaped with apples, and the fat round pillars which divided the church were skirted with oats and barley.

Almost everyone in the congregation had some hand in these things. Square-rumped farmers and ploughmen in chokers, old gardeners and poultry-keepers, they nodded and pointed and prodded each other to draw attention to what they had brought. The Church was older than its one foundation, was as old as man's life on earth. The seed of these fruits, and the seed of these men, still came from the same one bowl; confined to this valley and renewing itself here, it went back to the days of the Ice. Pride, placation, and the continuity of growth were what we had come to praise. And even where we sang, 'All is safely gathered in', knowing full well that some of Farmer Lusty's oats still lay rotting in the fields, the discrepancy didn't seem important.

I remember one particular Harvest Festival which perfectly summed up this feeling. I was not old enough then to be in the choir, and I was sitting beside Tony, who was three. It was his first Harvest Festival, but he'd heard much about it and his expectations were huge. The choir, with banners, was fidgeting in the doorway, ready to start its procession. Tony gazed with glittering eyes around him, sniffing the juicy splendours. Then, in a moment of silence, just before the organ crashed into the hymn, he asked loudly, 'Is there going to be drums?'

It was a natural question, innocent and true. For neither drums, nor cymbals, nor trumpets of brass would have seemed out of place at that time.

THE DEATH OF the Squire was not the death of the church, though they drew to their end together. He died, and the Big House was sold by auction and became a Home for Invalids. The lake silted up, the swans flew away, and the great pike choked in the reeds. With the Squire's hand removed, we fell apart – though we were about to do so anyway. His servants dispersed and went into the factories. His nephew broke up the estate.

Fragmentation, free thought, and new excitements, came now to intrigue and perplex us. The first young couple to get married in a registry office were roundly denounced from the pulpit. 'They who play with fire shall be consumed by fire!' stormed the vicar. 'Ye mark my words!' Later he caught me reading *Sons and Lovers* and took it away and destroyed it. This may well have been one of his last authoritative gestures. A young apologist succeeded him soon.

Meanwhile the old people just dropped away – the white-whiskered, gaitered, booted and bonneted, ancient-tongued last of their world, who thee'd and thou'd both man and beast, called young girls 'damsels', young boys 'squires', old men 'masters', the Squire himself 'He', and who remembered the Birdlip stagecoach. Kicker Harris, the old coachman, with his top-hat and leggings, blew away like a torn-out page. Lottie Escourt, peasant shoot of a Norman lord, curled up in her relics and died. Others departed with hardly a sound. There was old Mrs Clissold, who sometimes called us for errands: 'Thee come up our court a minute, squire; I wants thee to do I a mission.' One ran to the shop to buy her a packet of bull's-eyes and was rewarded in the customary way. Bull's-eye in cheek, she'd sink back in her chair and dismiss one with a sleepy nod. 'I ain't nurn a aypence about I just now – but Mrs Crissole'll recollect 'ee . . .' We wrote her off as the day's good deed, and she died still recollecting us.

Now the last days of my family, too, drew near, beginning with the courting of the girls.

I remember very clearly how it started. It was summer, and we boys were sitting on the bank watching a great cloud of smoke in the sky.

A man jumped off his bike and cried, 'It's the boiler-works!' and we ran up the hill to see it.

There was a fire at the boiler-works almost every year. When we got there we found it a particularly good one. The warehouse, as usual, was sheathed in flame, ceilings and floors fell in, firemen shouted, windows melted like icicles, and from inside the building one heard thundering booms as the boilers started crashing about. We used up a lot of the day at this, cheering each toppling chimney.

When we got back to the village, much later in the evening, we saw a strange man down in our garden. We studied him from a distance with some feeling of shock. No one but neighbours and visiting relations had ever walked there before. Yet this ominous stranger was not only wandering free, he was being accompanied by all our women.

We rushed down the bank and burst roughly upon them, to find everyone crack-jawed with politeness. Our sisters cried La! when they saw us coming, and made us welcome as though we'd been round the world. Marjorie was particularly soft and loving, the others beamed anxiously at us; Mother, though not smart, was in her best black dress, and the stranger was twisting his hat.

'These are our brothers,' said Marjorie, grabbing two of us close to her bosom. 'This is Jackie and Loll, and that one's Tone. They're all of them terrible bad.'

There was nervous laughter and relief at this, as though several dark ghosts had been laid. We smirked and wriggled, aped and showed off, but couldn't think what was going on. In fact, the day of that boiler-works fire marked a beacon in the life of our girls. It was the day when their first young man came courting, and this stranger was he, and he was Marjorie's, and he opened a path through the garden.

He was handsome, curly-haired, a builder of barges, very strong, and entirely acceptable. His name was Maurice, and we boys soon approved him and gave him the run of the place. He was followed quite quickly by two other young men, one each for Dorothy and Phyllis. Dorothy got Leslie, who was a shy local scoutmaster, at least until he met her; Phyllis in turn produced Harold the Bootmaker, who had fine Latin looks, played the piano by ear, and sang songs about old-fashioned mothers. Then Harold, our brother, got the infection too, mended our chairs, re-upholstered the furniture, and brought home a girl for himself.

At these strokes our home life changed forever; new manners and notions crept in; instead of eight in the kitchen there were now a round dozen, and so it stayed till the girls started marrying. The young men called nightly, with candles in jars, falling headlong down our precipitous bank; or came pushing their bikes on summer evenings, loitering with the girls in the lanes; or sat round the fire talking slowly of work; or sat silent, just being there; while the sewing-machine hummed, and Mother rambled, and warm ripples of nothing lapped round them. They were wary of Mother, unsure of her temper, though her out-bursts were at the world, not people. Leslie was tactful and diffident, giving short sharp laughs at her jokes. Maurice often lectured her on 'The Working Man Today', which robbed her of all understanding. Phyl's Harold would sometimes draw up to the piano, strike the keys with the strength of ten, then charm us all by bawling 'Because' or 'An Old Lady Passing By'.

Then there was cheese and cocoa, and 'Goodnight all', and the first one got up to leave. There followed long farewells by the back-kitchen door, each couple taking their turn. Those waiting inside had to bide their time. 'Our Doth! Ain't you finished yet?' 'Shan't be a minute.' Yum-yum, kiss-kiss. 'Well, hurry up do! You're awful.' Five more minutes of silence outside, then Marge shakes the latch on the door. 'How much longer, our Doth? You been there all night. There's some got to work tomorrow.' 'All right, don't get ratty. He's just off now. Night-night, my beautiful bab.' One by one they departed; we turned down the lights, and the girls heaved themselves to bed.

Sundays, or Bank Holidays, were day-long courtships, and then the lovers were all over us. When it rained it was hopeless and we just played cards, or the boy friends modelled for dress-making. When fine perhaps Mother would plan a small treat, like a picnic in the woods.

I remember a sweltering August Sunday. Mother said it would be nice to go out. We would walk a short mile to a nice green spot and boil a kettle under the trees. It sounded simple enough, but we knew better. For Mother's picnics were planned on a tribal scale, with huge preparations beforehand. She flew round the kitchen issuing orders and the young men stood appalled at the work. There were sliced cucumbers and pots of paste, radishes, pepper and salt, cakes and buns and macaroons, soup-plates of bread and butter, jam, treacle, jugs of milk, and several fresh-made jellies.

The young men didn't approve of this at all, and muttered it was blooming mad. But with a 'You carry that now, there's a dear boy', each of us carried something. So we set off at last like a frieze of Greeks bearing gifts to some woodland god – Mother, with a tea-cloth over her head, gathering flowers as she went along, the sisters following with cakes and bread, Jack with the kettle, Tony with the salt, myself with a jug of milk; then the scowling youths in their blue serge suits carrying the jellies in open basins – jellies which rapidly melted in the sun and splashed them with yellow and rose. The young men swapped curses under their breath, brother Harold hung back in shame, while Mother led the way with prattling songs determined to make the thing go.

She knew soon enough when people turned sour and moved mountains to charm them out of it, and showed that she knew by a desperate gaiety and by noisy attacks on silence.

'Now come along, Maurice, best foot forward, mind how you go, tee-hee. Leslie! just look at those pretty what-d'you-call'ems – those what's-is – *aren't* they a picture? I said Leslie, look, aren't they pretty, my dear? Funny you don't know the name. Oh, isn't it a scrumptious day, tra-la? Boys, isn't it a scrumptious day?'

Wordy, flustered, but undefeated, she got us to the woods at last. We were ordered to scatter and gather sticks and to build a fire for the kettle. The fire smoked glumly and stung our eyes, the young men sat round like martyrs, the milk turned sour, the butter fried on the bread, cake-crumbs got stuck to the cucumber, wasps seized the treacle, the kettle wouldn't boil, and we ended by drinking the jellies.

As we boys would eat anything, anywhere, none of this bothered us much. But the young courting men sat on their spread silk-handkerchiefs and gazed at the meal in horror. 'No thanks, Mrs Lee. I don't think I could. I've just had me dinner, ta.'

They were none of them used to such disorder, didn't care much for open-air picnics – but most of all they were wishing to be away with their girls, away in some field or gully, where summer and love would be food enough, and an absence of us entirely.

LAURIE LEE was born in Gloucestershire in 1914 and raised in the village of Slad. At the age of nineteen he said goodbye to his mother and left home to walk to London. Over the years that followed he worked as an office clerk, labourer, poet, journalist and documentary film-maker. He also wrote and travelled extensively in Spain.

Cider With Rosie, from which this Mini is taken, was first published in 1959. It was an instant bestseller and became a beloved memoir of childhood and the English countryside for millions of people worldwide. Laurie Lee wrote the book over ten years and it changed his life. He was able to become a full-time writer and to buy a cottage in his home village of Slad.

RECOMMENDED BOOKS BY LAURIE LEE:

Cider With Rosie
A Rose for Winter
As I Walked Out One Midsummer Morning

Still having dreams of Summer?

Liberty
VIRGINIA WOOLF

VINTAGE MINIS

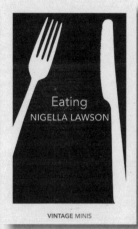

Eating
NIGELLA LAWSON

VINTAGE MINIS

Swimming
ROGER DEAKIN

VINTAGE MINIS

Drinking
JOHN CHEEVER

VINTAGE MINIS

VINTAGE MINIS

The Vintage Minis bring you the world's greatest writers on the experiences that make us human. These stylish, entertaining little books explore the whole spectrum of life – from birth to death, and everything in between. Which means there's something here for everyone, whatever your story.

Desire	Haruki Murakami
Love	Jeanette Winterson
Babies	Anne Enright
Language	Xiaolu Guo
Motherhood	Helen Simpson
Fatherhood	Karl Ove Knausgaard
Summer	Laurie Lee
Jealousy	Marcel Proust
Sisters	Louisa May Alcott
Home	Salman Rushdie
Race	Toni Morrison
Liberty	Virginia Woolf
Swimming	Roger Deakin
Work	Joseph Heller
Depression	William Styron
Drinking	John Cheever
Eating	Nigella Lawson
Psychedelics	Aldous Huxley
Calm	Tim Parks
Death	Julian Barnes

vintageminis.co.uk